For That Day Only

For That Day Only

Poems by

Grace Schulman

THE SHEEP MEADOW PRESS
RIVERDALE-ON-HUDSON, NEW YORK

All inquiries and permission requests should be addressed to:
The Sheep Meadow Press, Post Office Box 1345,
Riverdale-on-Hudson, New York 10471.

Designed and Typeset by the Sheep Meadow Press.
Distributed by the Sheep Meadow Press.

Printed on acid-free paper in the United States. This book meets the
guidelines for permanence and durability of the Committee on Production
Guidelines for Book Longevity of the Council on Library Resources.

Library of Congress Cataloging-in-Publication Data

Schulman, Grace.
      For that day only / Grace Schulman.
      p.   cm.
      ISBN 1-878818-29-5 (cloth) $19.95
      I. Title.
PS3569.C538F67   1994
811.54--dc20   94-16633
                                                                    CIP

Second Prnting 1994

The Sheep Meadow Press gratefully acknowledges grants from the National
Endowment for the Arts and the New York State Council on the Arts which
helped in the publication of this book.

BOOKS BY GRACE SCHULMAN

POETRY

For That Day Only: Poems
Hemispheres: Poems
Burn Down the Icons: Poems

CRITICISM AND TRANSLATION

Marianne Moore: The Poetry of Engagement
At the Stone of Losses: Poems by T. Carmi
Songs of Cifar (with Ann Zavala),
    by Pablo Antonio Cuadra
Editor, *Ezra Pound*

ACKNOWLEDGMENTS

Some of these poems appeared originally in the following publications, to whose editors grateful acknowledgment is made:

Antaeus: "Expulsion."
Boulevard: "False Move," "Home Movie," "The Present Perfect."
A Celebration for Stanley Kunitz on His Eightieth Birthday: "Carrion."
Forward: "Footsteps on Lower Broadway."
Grand Street: "Rescue in Pescallo."
The Kenyon Review: "For That Day Only," "New Netherland, 1654."
The New Republic: "Julian of Norwich," "Two Trees."
The New Yorker: "Notes from Underground: W. H. Auden on the
    Lexington Avenue IRT."
The Paris Review: "Bestiaries."
Pequod: "Site:"
Pivot: "Somewhere in Brittany."
Poetry: "After the Division," "'Straight Talk, Straight as the Greek,'"
    "The Wedding."
Theology Today: "El Greco's 'St. James, the Less.'"
The Western Humanities Review: "The Movie," "The Button Box."
The Yale Review: "Easter in Bellagio."

"After the Division" also appeared in *To Woo and to Wed.*
"False Move" and "Rescue in Pescallo" also appeared in *Decade: New
    Letters, 1980-90.*
"For That Day Only" also appeared in *Walk On the Wild Side:
    Contemporary Urban Poetry.*
"Julian of Norwich" also appeared in *Oxford Poetry.*

The author wishes to thank the Corporation of Yaddo, the MacDowell Colony, and the Rockefeller Foundation at Bellagio, where many of these poems were written, and Baruch College, C.U.N.Y., for its continuing encouragement and support.

For my husband, Jerry

CONTENTS

4

5

The world, — this shadow of the soul, or *other
me,* — lies wide around.

— Ralph Waldo Emerson

Harrow the house of the dead; look shining at
New styles of architecture, a change of heart.

— W. H. Auden

1

FOR THAT DAY ONLY

New York, June 11, 1883

Daybreak, and she left her poppyseed roll
to follow them as they walked through the city
carrying the dead child, her fourth brother

born in their new world. Sunlight revealed
a stark, unbending man; a hawklike woman
in a stiff wig, wearing a nubby shawl;

and Uncle Ben, with the bouncing silver watch,
their only kin. Now they exhausted sorrow
by humming sacred phrases in the trek

from Pitt Street to the Brooklyn cemetery.
Her mother glanced at her, the oldest daughter,
who had rocked beside the stove and read to him

English words that rang like bits of praise
fallen out of prayer, from Homer's tales
of a nymph whose breath filled sails, images

a storyteller scooped out of a basket
that pierced the morning fog, then disappeared,
like a cat's firecoal eyes — alive, but never

as real as asphalt on this long day.
She never saw the film inside his throat,
and had to be pried away when she tried to breathe

life into his mouth. Just before dawn,
she saw their forms as she sang to the baby's pillow;
hands stroked her hand and led her to the march.

And now, how bright they were. How, well — how *visible*.
How steep her father's shoulders. The same light
that warmed them froze gray towers in what was

her first view of the city beyond the neighborhood,
beyond the block. Seeing everything,
trying to see nothing at either side,

she almost smiled at trees, jerked back her head,
remembering herself, and hid her eyes
when she saw a woman speed a bicycle

as though about to rise up over the pavement
like a streetcar's horses that, though ponderous,
might break into a gallop in the wind.

Circles bloomed everywhere: a yellow ball
flew at a hedge; coaches had creaky wheels;
a white hoop, tapped with a stick, zoomed from behind.

There was a brown house with a tulip patch,
for just one family — or so a brass-star
policeman said, who ushered them through crowds

in City Hall Park, and waved at flags on buildings
with plate-glass shop windows. She tripped on loose
cobblestones, and where the streets were roads,

the ground marsh after a night of rain,
she danced and fell, her ankle-boots soaked through,
then clambered to the walk to watch a beetle

scurry toward some weeds grown through black gaps
in concrete rectangles. She tried to touch
the statue of a man in bronze that was mottled,

green-going black, with a beckoning,
historical hand, creased at its great wrist.
Longing to stop by a straw-hat cart near a girl

who tugged at a hatless woman with red real hair,
she pushed on to the harbor, where a gull
barely skimmed her head, and climbed the new

Brooklyn Bridge, her alley to the dead.
Chanting lines of the Psalms to secular tunes
that moved her — local streetcries, arias —

she studied the bearded man in front of her,
observed his set jaw, stirred to his praise,
and feared the tiny boy would grow as heavy

as a bag of stones by the time their journey ended.
Stalwart, proud, he held their grief to his chest
for that day only; moments after sunrise,

her mother had raised white arms and yielded up
the shapeless sack. Sun growing higher,
she knew that she, the oldest daughter,

would haul that ragged body even after
the procession ended, when they returned
by gaslight to their dim rooms, and, in fact,

whenever she walked alone in her new city —
brick-hard and vast, but never unredeeming —
the next day and the next one and the next.

THE MOVIE

One day I stumbled on a movie set
Of University Place: a surreal park,
A pointillist mews with gleaming iron gates,
Shuttered buildings hollow at the back,

Streetlights that would topple in a breeze.
Leaving my house, clutching the rubbery basket
I use for farmer's-market vegetables,
Gingerly, I walked into a street

Stripped of actual traffic, to discover
"Freshmen" chattering like orioles. A man
In canvas overalls, crowd choreographer,
Barked syllables in opposite directions,

And set us off, a passersby ballet
Whose paths were planned. Some watched for non-existent
Green lights; one woman nervously
Darted, jostling books from pseudo-students.

Then a flower vendor wheeled a wagon
Past us. An actor ran with outstretched arms,
Missed it and cursed it, green eyes so forlorn
I knew that he would follow those geraniums

Forever. And that was all the cameras
Reeled in that morning: one scene with the same
Brightness that had possessed me over the years
I sailed with Bette Davis in a storm

Of black-and-white, trailed Bogart's enemies
Who wear magenta neckties (colorized),
And wept through *Les Enfants du paradis*.
When the director let us go, I realized

That the protection of familiar things
Was limited. At best I was a stranger.
Undoubtedly, the market would be traveling
On wheels to another city, and the copy center

Delivered elsewhere, shelves and window panes.
Some crew would sandblast the "U.S. Government
Post Office" block letters, engraved in stone.
Seeing mica glitter on the pavement,

I scrutinized my neighbors for their real
Identities, and warily questioned every
Role. Under the sun's strobe, at my peril,
I staggered into an enamel sky,

Knowing my destiny would be geraniums,
Blood-red and quivering on a rickety wagon
I might never encounter, only watch them
Drop velvety petals as they rattled on.

THE PRESENT PERFECT

I saw the cells on tv, as they swam
up to the egg, tails lashing, and I heard
the wind-tunnel sound they make, the steady hum

of thousands, blind, threadlike, worn, but soaring
through waterfalls in their drive to live, move,
and set the egg revolving like a star.

For us, there was no miracle of birth.
No genes, no geniuses. And yet, OK,
we had other things: our work, our history

scrawled on Margaux labels and libretti,
and, after all, no cribs, no sticky plums,
no pulling paper napkins, one by one,

from a metal box, to mop up dumped ice cream.
But then again, no immortality:
in my religion, children to speak my name

after I am. No heir to your kindness,
your skill with a kite, your father's whimsey,
or to my mother's mother's diamond pin.

And yet, we had each other's silences;
freedom to wander with no fixed plan,
now fixed in photos of sylphs that resemble us,

peering down cliffs in Brittany at ragged boards
floated up from dinghies lost at sea,
searching for fish carved into chapels' altars,

spending our suns like out-of-date coins,
until we reached the present-perfect tense —
that have-been state where past and future merge:

We have been married thirty-four years.
I see the kids we were frisk on this lawn
in the late afternoon's unnameable light.

Too late for them, and for their unborn kids,
but not too late for us, here among cedars,
to praise the fires in rose petals on slate;

white rhododendrons, a fountain's rainbow.
I see the dot of you, meadows away,
that grows in sight as you pedal home;

your reddish hair and beard, now tarnished silver,
that once we wanted for a chromosome;
your silhouette in a Manet-like straw hat

as you bless your new astilbe: "Live and be well,"
casting aside your customary questions
for an irrational faith the plant will grow;

I hear your voice that calls me to see wildflowers
poking through gravel cracks in our neighbors' driveway,
slender but fortunate, built to last their day.

AFTER THE DIVISION

Here it is! In an unbleached photograph,
Plato's two halves of man-and-woman, cast
of our shadows, sliced and joined again: four arms,
four legs, two heads. Metallic, silver-gray,

that blade clicks from our feet at acute angles
from our bodies, then it becomes a gaunt,
barbarous giant and creeps toward the sea.
Below us, in the foreground, the white sand

is ruffled now by footsole indentations,
and you, above the tracks, a leggy matador,
brandish a towel the sun has gored blood-red.
You search the land; musing behind your shoulder,

I watch the ocean. After that sun fell,
we cracked apart. I listened for your silences
in clamorous voices; looked for your merest
accidental glance among the usual

predators. With quartz-clear eyes
you told me I looked lovely in a torn
dress, but questioned natural laws. Remember
the night you challenged probability,

tossing a coin to count one hundred heads
until the dawn, an enterprise that lulled
me, but held you fast. You never pondered
gravity, compelled instead by bonds

between revolving worlds and fallen apples.
Driven by what anemones are made of,
not by their names, calmly you insisted
that viruses have viruses, and cells

have dictionaries, and even memories.
With quiet fortitude and dour tenacity,
probing a cloud, examining a dahlia,
godless, you led me to my God. One day,

in solitude, I caught your stalky form
jack-knifed over a lean golden retriever,
and avenues spun like planets. There was time.
One night I watched El Greco's Cardinal

sprout your weedy beard. Still, there was time.
Unlike Dante's damned, who see the future,
but not the past, I reel in what there was,
and wish when we had marched on brittle leaves

to *L'Internationale*, that shadows drawn
into our forms at noon, were visible.
Tonight we walk under the same mimosa trees
and wonder why we severed then; creepers

hooked into oaks to live, we held too fast,
when earth and sun — all things, irregular —
converge and separate. We ask again
why we merged to want this moment now,

and see only the creature in the photograph
(though whether it has life, as you would say,
is philosophical, depending on
degrees of selfhood), but, in any case,

a being, torn in two, grown whole, the root
our bodies spring from, moves discreetly
toward the sea. After twelve years apart,
I watch its steely edges cut the sand,

and know it will glide, unseen, even when day
concludes. I wake with you and feel the sun
invent one shadow that starts out from us,
and know the time has come to begin our lives.

2

FOOTSTEPS ON LOWER BROADWAY

Grace Church's steeple still fishes the sky
over Broadway, and bobs up from the walker,
Walt Whitman's "lighthouse" on an "inland sea,"
crowded now but unsubmerged by towers,
and seen from building fronts that call up kings:
Renaissance columns, friezes, dormers, bellowing
gargoyles I've missed by never looking up.
I dogged him until his swaggering steps
merged with mine, and I ran into you —
a seething Hungarian immigrant, a Jew.

Hearing "the blab of the pave," I walked from the wharf's
wind-bent sloops and headed for Pfaff's
cave (now haunting a produce stand) to eat
with rowdies and squint at the theater crowd.
I waved at omnibus drivers — Pop Rice, Patsy Dee —
and elbowed by rings of stiff men in black coats
posing like unlighted streetlamps. How he
scowled at their boutonnieres, and touched his beard,
no "washes and razors" for him, nor for you —
an out-of-fashion immigrant, a Jew.

These great houses breathe under their sites.
Gaslight shadows flicker on walls at night.
See the razed opera house on Astor Place
where Badioli sang, and Mario.
For Whitman at St. Ann's, high Glorias
blended with deckhands' tunes on the Fulton ferry;
now, drifting over new talk on Broadway,
raw winds carry arias from *Lucia*
that Whitman heard, free-ticketed, and you,
gripping a spear, an immigrant Jew.

Whitman, in a synagogue on Crosby Street,
heard ancient vows in scenes "entirely new."
Men keened, their voices nameless deep-toned bells.
He wrote for the press: a "paneled wood" enclosure
held "sugar loaves" topped with glass and silver;
then, wrapped in white silk, the priest (he *thought*)
waved a parchment scroll. "The heart within
felt awed," he said, and his speech fell
under minor chords that enchanted you
when you were there, an immigrant, a Jew

who read the Law and knew the ritual.
On Pike Street, where your father was a cantor,
you sang the sacred hymns to melodies
from oratorios you'd heard in concert halls,
and once, a Sabbath chant, *Leha dodi*,
"Go, my beloved…" to a rollicking tune,
"There's One New York," struck up in a saloon.
Whitman woke to song; you crafted prayer,
whittling down the past to make it new
in your New York, an immigrant, a Jew.

In steamy rain, I zigzagged through your ghetto,
Orchard Street, Hester. Winter-melon bins
replace old pushcarts filled with knives and buttons;
on shop windows, brush-strokes read high-to-low,
not right-left, as your letters did, and now
graffiti on metal doors are calligraphic.
From here to City Hall you hiked, then on
to Washington Square's law school, looking back
on trees and weed-grown lots — all that you knew
of what was or would be, an immigrant Jew.

Move, move, move, to con brio scores
in your head. Praise all things fixed and loose.
Even when you can ride in horse-drawn cars,
walk, to feel unstuck cobbles through your soles,
to see leaves stuck to pebbled rectangles
like jewels in velvet bodices, to peer
from under elms at posters of Irving's *Lear*
and Olga Nethersole's *Camille*. In magic boots
dance on spangled streets that discover you
grateful to be an immigrant, a Jew.

Whitman you neither touched nor read, but here
men and women become one crowd and flow:
shoppers in sweats, kids with shrill radios,
temperance workers, livestock merchants, share
stagecoach clatter, trucks' din, vendors' whines,
and see towers rise: his, slate; yours, marble; mine,
Mondrians skyscrapers make of the sky.
On misty days, I trek to the port and see
twin water-gazers, he, slouching, and you,
shifting about, a restless immigrant Jew

observing stone cut sharp, cut round: angular
capitals, curved shields; faces of gods.
I gather years carved into stone arcades
and cast on cornices, solid as ancestry,
while I hear a man drum jazz on a kitchen pail.
For Henry James, a walker in your day
you never knew, these streets hummed, bristled, lay
open to change: buildings were words that die
in air; he called them "impudently new" —
as you were then, a prospering immigrant Jew.

I find the Statue of Liberty draped in black
for President Garfield's assassination,
just as you did when your parents packed
in Hungary for free schools. Diamonds shine
in the boat's spume. A castle in the bay!
I've had to shape them, for your past was gone
under new asphalt. Now I hoard stone griffins
and cast-iron numbers, "1 8 7 3,"
on red brick, combing history for you,
Grandfather Dave, an immigrant, a Jew.

NEW NETHERLAND, 1654

Pardon us for uttering a handful
or words in *any* language, so cut loose
are we from homes, and from His name that is still
nameless, blessed be He. We raised a prayer house —

that is, we broke new wood for one, but some
tough burned it, snarling: "Carve only stones for the dead."
Damp ground, no fire, no psalm we all remember.
But tall ships anchor here, and at low tide,

people with wheat-colored hair look out to sea,
just as we'd searched for land. "Pray if you must,"
my father said, "and when prayer fails, a story —
if it is all you have, will do." Months past,

we left Recife's force-worship laws in the Year
of *their* Lord, sixteen-hundred and fifty-four, for our new
world, old-country Amsterdam. Leagues seaward,
Spanish pirates slaughtered our scant crew,

and all that was left of us (friends wheezed
their last while they ragged us on) rose up on deck
and tossed our bags in the sea. We watched the wake
turn silver: kiddish wine cups, hanging bowls,

a candelabra for the promised altar,
carved pointers. Books' pages curled and sank,
prayer shawls ballooned, and, soaking, spiraled downward.
Just as we stared, again we heard swords clank —

a French ship, the St. Catherine (her prow had shone
gold on a gray horizon) came to our
port side and rescued us. In that commotion
on deck, we crouched below — not out of fear,
I swear, but stunned by luminous words

that echoed oddly — beautifully — like lightning
flickering through palls of thickset clouds.
A jaunty captain rasped to us in hiding:

"Where are you bound?"
                              "Amsterdam. Old country."
"Where ?"
              "Amsterdam."
                              "Antilles?"
                                            "No, Amsterdam."
"Yes, yes. Nieuw *Am*sterdam. I'll see
you get there safely." He meant well, bless him.

St. Catherine sailed to land at its tip no larger
than a meadow, fanned out at its sides:
Manhattan Island. Our new master,
Stuyvesant, lashed us with phrases, *wheffs*, *guzzads*,

that stung but were not fathomed, mercifully,
when we came on a Sabbath, more than twenty
men, women, a baby born at sea.
Still cursing, he let us land, and heard our praise,

then disappeared among lank citizens
with faded skin who stride to the bay and brood
on water that we trust and dread, and listen
to tales unstamped by laws and never sacred.

THE BUTTON BOX

A sea animal stalked its prey
slithering under her bed, and gorged
on buttons torn from castaways;
ever unsated, it grew large

until it became a deity
spewing out buttons in a fire
of brass for blazers, delft or ruby
for shirts — and dangerous. You'd hear

it snarl when the beds were being made.
It ate stray pins and shot out poison.
But mother, who stuffed its wooden frame,
scooped up waterfalls of suns,

enamel moons, clocks, cameos,
carved pinwheels, stars, tiny "Giottos,"
peacocks strutting out at sundown,
FDR's profile, flags of Britain,

silver helmets, all with missions.
Mother sewed ballerinas set
in circles on your satin dress,
onyx buttons that would join

you, collar-to-hood, at graduation;
she would find in the creature's lair
"bones" of an army officer,
"pearls" of a war-bride's dressing gown;

nights when the radio hissed *dive bombers*
mother dreamed that she could right
the world again by making sure
you had your buttons, sewed on tight.

HOME MOVIE

Just then the squeaky camera caught
a sun crystal that haloed trees,
blurred fences, light dousing the light,
then twitched, and quivered into focus,

as I entered the child I was,
primped for the film in a ruffled smock,
touching the big hepaticas
I'd never seen in Central Park,

then pivoting to see my mother's
long arms arc through foamy water,
stroke by feathery stroke, and soar,
her white cap lost then found in glare,

and I, gasping in pride, in awe,
recalled a newsreel's dreadful flare
as warplanes fired at refugees,
mother and son, *people like us*,

then watched her rise up at the shore,
step to a tango, snap a towel,
and ran to her, eyes wide with all
I'd know of perfect form — and fear.

SITE:

The absence of a house. A negative image,
listed at wrong addresses in the guidebooks;
in fact, invisible. Still, it invites
what negative capability the heart

can muster — not simply to observe
the sun's glare on a jet's wing before sunrise,
but in dark rooms to hear a lost friend's laughter.
Take the house at 19 Washington Square,

the one with no brass plaque that claims
it's the site of a house in a book by Henry James.
When the late sun reddens the auburn bricks,
stare until stone steps turn to white marble,

Ionic columns flank the wooden door,
and frayed roses in the yard become
bold peonies restrained by iron fences
handwrought with lyres, Greek frets, acanthus leaves.

Peer through needlepoint lace above a balcony
and find a woman at a writing-table
in a red gown and shawl chosen so "they,
and not she, would look well," and know

that things survive in their sites, in the ghosts of houses,
linger in the incandescent images
of what we imagine has occurred: the parlor
after the guests have gone, the broken phrase

somebody whistled once; the theater's curtain
that holds the mark of the dancer's perilous leap
skyward — the flexed plié, the twist and spin
so high it seemed he would never descend.

THE TER CLOS,*

a gap-toothed sign,
hovers over what were glass doors,
a ticket booth, a list of shows and hours,
an entrance now bricked-up and plastered
with torn posters
of Fields and Chaplin.

Black letters flake
and swirl with leaflets, clipped cartoons,
newspapers, gold labels, crinkly wrappers,
bills from cafés, usually dense
and wordier,
here after dark.

Just before dawn,
the *ter clos* unfolds metal legs and slides
down from its canopy and tells of scenes
played and replayed; a dancer glides;
a brigantine
dips on the ocean,

challenging time.
The gloomy *ter clos* will not hear
losses are living images that change
into one figure, then another:
the perfect face
ripples on water.

*Originally, the sign read, "Theater Closed."

It grits chipped teeth
and strides past settler's lanes now zoned
for skyscrapers, scorning shops just opened,
looks icily at hedges that are blooming
too late for spring,
retraces its path,

and climbs back on
the stone façade, and cries: "My warehouse has angels
that whoosh out through fissures in the walls;
my soundtracks are arias of spheres
that for dull ears
are too high, too fine."

The *ter clos* fumes
at the story of the world's beginning:
of how God hushed his coloratura thrones,
his mezzo archangels, to hear men, women —
his creatures — sing,
sometimes off-tune.

CROSSING THE SQUARE

Squinting through eye-slits in our balaclavas,
we lurch across Washington Square Park
hunched against the wind, two hooded figures
caught in the monochrome, carrying sacks

of fruit, as we've done for years. The frosted, starch-
stiff sycamores make a lean Christmas tree
seem to bulk larger, tilted under the Arch,
and still lit in three colors. Once in January,

we found a feather here and stuffed the quill
in twigs to recall that jay. The musical fountain
is here, its water gone, a limestone circle
now. Though rap succeeds the bluegrass strains

we've played in it, new praise evokes old sounds.
White branches mimic visions of past storms;
some say they've heard ghosts moan above this ground,
once a potter's field. No two stones are the same,

of course: the drums, the tawny pears we hold,
are old masks for new things. Still, in a world
where fretted houses with façades are leveled
for condominiums, not much has altered

here. At least it's faithful to imagined
views. And, after all, we know the sycamore
will screen the sky in a receding wind.
Now, trekking home through grit that's mounting higher,

faces upturned to test the whirling snow,
in new masks, we whistle to make breath-clouds form
and disappear, and form again, and O,
my love, there's sun in the crook of your arm.

NOTES FROM UNDERGROUND:
W. H. AUDEN ON THE LEXINGTON AVENUE IRT

Hunched in a corner seat, I'd watch him pass
riders who gaped at headlines: "300 DEAD,"
and, in their prized indifference to all
others, were unaware he was one who heard
meter in that clamor of wheels on rails.

Some days I took the local because he did:
He sank down into plastic, his bruised sandals
no longer straining with the weight of him;
there, with the frankness of the unacquainted,
I studied his face, a sycamore's bark

with lichen poking out of crevices.
His eyes lifted over my tattered copy
of his *Selected Poems*, then up to where
they drilled new windows in the car and found,
I guessed, tea roses and a healing fountain.

All memories are echoes: some whisper,
others roar, as this does. Dazed by war,
I, who winced at thunder, knew that train
screeched "DISASTER!" How it jolted and veered,
station after station, chanting *Kyrie*

eleison, while metal clanged on metal,
and bulbs went dim. Peering at tracks, I heard,
"Still persuade us to rejoice." I glimpsed
a worn sandal, turned, and then my eyes
met his eyes that rayed my underworld.

3

GOD'S LETTERS

When God thought up the world,
the alphabet letters
whistled in his crown,
where they were engraved
with a pen of fire,
each wanting to begin
the story of Creation.

S said, I am Soul.
I can Shine out
from within your creatures.
God replied, I know that,
but you are Sin, too.

L said, I am Love,
and I brush away malice.
God rejoined, yes,
but you are Lie,
and falsehood is not
what I had in mind.

P said, I am Praise,
and where there's a celebration,
I Perform
in my Purple coat.
Yes, roared God,
but at the same time,
you are Pessimism —
the other side of Praise.

And so forth.

All the letters
had two sides or more.
None was pure.
There was a clamor
in paradise, words,
syllables, shouting
to be seen and heard
for the glory
of the new heavens and earth.

God fell silent,
wondering,
how can song
rise from that commotion.

Rather than speculate,
God chose B,
who had intoned,
Bashfully, Boldly,
Blessed is *his* name.

And he made A
first in the Alphabet
for admitting, I am All —
a limitation
and a possibility.

BESTIARIES

1. ANIMALS

Before God created people,
he made animals,
unnamed and marvelous,
that sheltered the weak.
What later would be called
the leviathan
had fins so large
they hid the sun,
and eyes that lit up the sea.
It swallowed only fish
that leaped into its mouth,
spouted water
to frighten sharks,
and shed skins
to cover the poor.
The ziz, ruler of birds,
foresaw battles
and sang with angels;
its eggs, when broken,
flooded cities
and crushed cedars.
There were gentle dolphins,
fireproof salamanders,
shining ravens,
sly foxes, and unicorns
that cured the sick.
They showed us how to live;
best of all, the grasshopper
that trilled all summer long
before it died.

2. THEY, TOO

After Lewis Thomas

They, too, can tell us what we are,
not like the phoenix, that rises in ashes,
nor by their valor, like the ki-lin,

with its stag body and silver horn,
but because they take things in.
I mean the *myxotricha paradoxa*,

a protozoan made of spirochetes,
organelles, and more besides;
the *mitochondria*, assembled from

bacteria bits; the *blepharisma*,
that eats its neighbors. Unbeautiful,
their names unresonant, they fuse

with other cells, merge, lean, depend;
they show us we rent, share, occupy each other,
and never own, not even ourselves.

Praise them. They will shine like jewels
on the stained-glass windows of cathedrals
along with lambs and birds, rabbits and deer.

3. STONE DEMONS

Throw back your head and see them
hunt you down Amsterdam
with pop eyes, knifeblade ears,
gaps weathered into scars,
mouths that cry and drain
waterfalls of rain.

Gargoyles. Bas-reliefs
worn smooth as buffalo nickels.
And carved beasts — no, not beasts
but pied horrors: animals,
men and women, torn
then tacked together again.

Hear them shriek and howl.
One springs from a cornice,
another squats on a wall,
a third has wings, fishtail
and hooves, all at once
to fly, swim, leap and prance.

Cross streets, turn down alleys;
they'll spy you blocks away.
Sages with leafy beards,
kings with fangs, goat ears,
act out court murder scenes
blooded by falling suns.

Hybrid monsters teach us
waking and dreams are one:
our fears, urges and loves
sit high on towers of sandstone,
and poke up from the flat
bedrock of the heart.

EXPULSION

Half-rotten, half-sweet,
it lay on the ground for days
before I tried it,

and offered another
to my love, who said,
"I've never liked apples."

When I walked on,
he ate it, core and all.
And that's when it began.

We bought enough Rome Beauties
to make apple marmalade
and apple chutney —

then curries, soufflés,
pirozhki.
We grew restless,

even before the storm
cut off our water supply,
and winds lopped the elm

that cracked over telephone wire.
I remember
how in mild air

the sun lit the sheep laurel
and fell, along with quiet.
He called the perennials

by names once unfamiliar to us,
each with a resonance:
monkshood, purple iris,

foxglove, nightshade;
some we tended,
others grew wild,

recurring gifts.
But all was not right.
There were shrill insects,

scorpions, snaky vines
that twisted up cedars
and strangled white pines.

Here in the city,
things are less clear;
a rickety

ambulance snorts,
carrying the half-dead —
a pedestrian shot

during a robbery —
while toddlers embrace
twenty blocks away.

That square of street
not covered with grime
glitters in moonlight.

My love does not
give names to anything.
Instead, he falls silent

before a grove
of trees among buildings.
We cherish what little we have:

one side is bright,
the other dark.
We praise it.

TWO TREES

For David and Rhonda

Ancient borassus palms, masculine and feminine,
rise on this coast as they soared in Eden,

and yearn to join yet stand, earth, sky between them.
See them now, after the storm —

call it a whirlwind, or someone's cross phrase —
cracked the mangos' trunks, but spared these trees.

Each closes leafy fans above hard wood
that wraps the visionary self inside.

In a Van Eyck painting, man and wife are seen
and see: a convex mirror throws back curtains,

well-wishers, outside the viewer's province;
and, in a Beckett play, a man listens

to himself on a reel-to-reel recorder
speaking of a brighter, but unwanted, summer.

So the self gathers, multiplies, alone.
In this replanted Eden, newly grown

palms breathe free, unbent by other palms,
and bear fruit when they are ready, in their time.

FALSE MOVE

Hearing a thud, as though a ball had struck
my window pane, seeing a feathery mass
cling to the spot, I peered outside, fearfully
braced for some creature, writhing or inert.

It was a grackle, changing glass to air.
Dead still, the bird was on his feet. Too dazed
to fear my hand, he tilted a stiff head,
opened a knifelike beak but made no sound,

hunched an iridescent back. He's done for:
that polished purple, ebony and brown
will sink. With glassy eyes, he saw a clearing
larger than his cage of air allowed,

tested its limits, darted as though worlds
could bend. My ground is cumbrous earth that sun
can fire, storms erode. Those silver hills
beyond the hemlocks actually are mountains:

I've scaled their ledges, narrowly escaping
grooves. One step too far, one double image
can kill, I knew, and faltered. Then the bird
lowered his nape, compressed his body, flew.

4

THE WEDDING

Late spring in Caesaria, Herod's harbor,
now a city of Roman ruins, quiet
but for gull cries in the whitehot light
of midday. People gather at the shore

as if to see a sword dance, to hear drums
and dagger-beats on shields — the pre-biblical
rites of this region — not the nuptials
of military lovers: agile, slim

army border-guards on active duty
wearing pearl-white wedding costumes, she,
satin and lace, he, linen, stiffly
pressed. Seeming too young to fight *or* marry,

they pose for photographs, the sea exploding
on rocks, and, shoes cast off, run on hot sand
to the marriage canopy, a covering
to cast off demons. It snaps in high wind,

their sacred roof, a dazzling cotton
embroidered prayer-shawl whose supporting poles
are rifles held by three men and a woman
in combat fatigues. There, before them all,

a rabbi intones the seven benedictions,
offers wine, hears vows and blesses them,
and blesses children who sing psalms. At sundown,
when the bridal pair change into uniforms,

a shot rings out. A woman screams and falls.
Three of the groom's attendants grab the rifles
that held the canopy, fall to the ground
at the stammer of guns, rub faces with wet sand,

and, shouldering their weapons, run to the sea
firing at men who creep out of a dinghy
that's dragged aground. One of the intruders,
his buoyant gait so like the bride's

that he seems an invited cousin, drops to the shore,
face down. Another stranger staggers
a few yards, bleeding, his stubby fingers
frozen on his gun. Bodies pitch forward,

arms and legs flail. Silence. White garments strewn
like a book's blown pages, the groom bends down
to lift the prayer-shawl that lies, torn,
mud-splattered. He folds it, kisses it, then

flings his red beret to the darkening
sand. Leading his bride to a small car,
he turns back for a time, as though to hear,
through mounting wave-sounds, what the children sang.

SOMEWHERE IN BRITTANY

Sputtering on the autoroute, our Fiat
halted by a roadsign that shrugged "Laval:
50 kilometers," with squared-off shoulders.
              Then, scrawled on cardboard

nailed to a post, with black conflicting arrows,
"Mervan Mignac." Like hermit crabs that leave
their rented shells, we sidled out of ours, in
              hope of a gas pump,

and coaxed the car toward the place. Not quite a village,
not on the map's blue veins that told us our fortune,
but somewhere in Brittany, it shone before us,
              empty at noon for

two hours or more, a miniature lost under
thickets of trees at dusk for a century,
promising citizens who might surface through asphalt
              like stubborn flowers.

Visions of reaching Paris gone, we shrugged, grinned,
parked the auto by a bleak repair shop,
and sank in a meadow where no bird or rabbit
              rustled the dry leaves.

A Romanesque church stood in a tiny square
(could it contain frescoes of doves and angels?)
and called us, turned us away, and called us,
              turned us away, as

bells pealed, brawled, pealed, brawled, for it was bolted
like everything else in that sleeping parish.
Suddenly then a lank man strode shadowless
              under the hot sun

carrying roses, a baguette, Brie in a basket
— his cornucopia of faith — rapped loudly,
fiercely, unrelenting, on the frog-colored
               door of a stucco

house in a thundering silence at midday
until a lock clicked, and the door swung open.
There in the dark hall, a woman, a man's
               hand on her shoulder,

waited. The thin interloper muttered
while we, strangers, turned into friends who pleaded
for him unhearing what he desired, or
               why he desired —

we, aliens, our armor now a plane tree's
inching shade outside a steamy enclosure,
stirred for a man who stood unhoused when that door
               slammed with a loud thud

on him, on us, on things that exit, saddened,
from lifeless husks to life. At first, he smarted
on steps and hid bright eyes, blotched cheeks, and then
               gathered his roses,

leaped up and bounded away. When his arms faded
from view, all we could see were rose petals
scattered on black soil, gleaming like shells some
               creature had sloughed off.

JULIAN OF NORWICH

Warped in the window-diamonds of my cell,
distorted, outsize primroses unfold:
I see all manner of things that shall be well.

Eyeless men with plague-sores come to chapel,
hungry, with blood-soaked poultices, and cold.
Warped in the window-diamonds of my cell,

they lurch and fall, inert. Another dead bell.
Their king gone, my King blesses (dressed in gold,
I see), all manner of things that shall be well.

Hermits recoil. If I were to foretell
doom, monks would believe. Instead, I'm called
warped. In the window-diamonds of my cell

are men who know Black Death and wars, and tell
of starless night, and will until I'm old,
I see. All manner of things that shall be well

deceive: dense glass in quarrel panes can spell
disaster, lunacy. Faces are bold,
warped in the window-diamonds of my cell.
I see all manner of things that shall be well.

EASTER IN BELLAGIO

Even as earth rises here, as jonquils,
hepaticas and crocuses lift skyward,
I am amazed at things that fall: camellia
petals surround the tree in a scarlet wheel;
a cypress sheds dry needles and reveals
lyre-shaped branches. In this country, rain
on the lakes is snow that dazzles mountains.
The south wind brings a phosphorous mist that blends
rock and water into one dull mirror
whose chiseled images cannot be seen.

Master of laurel, craftsman of beginnings,
watercolorist of altering light:
surely as things fade to live, and loss
makcs trees grow green, just as the bells
of San Giacomo toll the hours and die,
then echo for miles in harbor towns,
the heart falls, rising. From clay-colored houses
set in these hills, the people stagger down
winding paths only to climb stone steps,
blood-colored at dawn, carrying palms.

RESCUE IN PESCALLO

Neither do I believe in miracles,
although at times an actual homely image
can lift the eyes and the expectations. Pale,
dark-haired, severe, a woman from the village

of Pescallo said a statue of Christ
had washed up on these shores and startled schoolboys
who called some local men, fishing for trout.
They listened closely, as for a drowned man's cries

of life, and stared at the figure, carved in oak,
the body painted white, the hair and beard
black. They hauled it up and carried it
to the Church of San Giacomo, a good

kilometer away, where she'd last seen it, lying
under a fresco of the Deposition
ascribed to Perugino. "Now the painting
may be a replica, but it's clear that wooden

figure is unique, for what it is,"
she said, and frowned. "You know the yellow-white
scant flower, the anemone? It grows
among these stones, in shade. So too, that

carving bobbed on the waves and steered through ice.
I guess it came as flotsam, possibly
junked, along with boards that had been pews,
cast out of a ruined chapel in a nearby

harbor on the lake." Rapt, she continued,
"Or, perhaps, in transit, it fell overboard,
not to be retrieved until, by God,
it loomed up here." The woman halted, stirred

by some dark memory, and threw a tarpaulin
over her stone sarcophagus. A sculptor
who modeled snaky forms, her studio once
a stable on a villa near the water,

she led me down an aisle of cypresses
that trapped a cloud, and would, until the wind
rose. It seemed we glided in a tapestry
of towers and doves, all things enlarged beyond

normal scale in the clear air. I gathered
the statue baffled her. She dismissed events
that wanted proof, and knew the dense-grained wood,
the size and weight, the tides, the precise moment

it surfaced, but she inferred that it had come
— like pen-strokes in her drawings for sarcophagi —
from a chillier place than she could fathom,
try as she did. Returning to the story,

she said, "That day, the south wind we call *breva*
brought ghostly mist that dimmed the bald horizon,
welding sky and water into metal.
In fog, the people saw the mud-smirched, lean

Christ walk through their spiraling thin streets,
hoisted on the shoulders of two fishermen,
staggering, really, head, nailed feet, and torso
one seesaw plank that passed the shops, the one

waterfront caffe and the pier. It sidled
onto the Via Garibaldi, where
it nearly grazed a bench when one man buckled
and fell. Seeing the statue waver

and lean a bit, clerks left their shops, doors open,
to set it right. Determined caribinieri,
who'd seen the pallid relic pass their station
in mist, stopped traffic. Blank-faced passersby

joined a kind of ritual parade that went
to the church door, where nuns and merchants set
the mottled body, scrubbed, dabbed with new paint,
on a slab inside the crypt." The woman thought

none of the villagers knew what had happened,
in their minds' eyes, or were the better for it.
"They're all retarded cousins in Pescallo,"
she muttered to her watch, an hour late.

She had shunned Daylight Time, since, as a girl,
she heard Il Duce rule it into law;
she doubted love, distrusted friendship, grateful
simply to look, bear witness and withdraw.

Charcoal-haired, with eyes both fixed and empty,
and moon-blanched skin, she carved heads in the style
of Donatello, then, in Milan, she woke
to obscure archbishops' tombs in purple

marble, amazed at life flesh-eaters gave,
and made sarcophagus relief. Tenaciously,
she chiseled Hindu deities, brave
princes and governors in vaults. Not airy

avatars, but weighty men and women
danced on her coffins. Curiously, they changed,
each more itself when its contours were gone
to others in the clusters she arranged.

Finishing one sculpture, then another,
she ticked off years, then bent under great losses.
Lifeless as crystal, she intoned that after
her son had died of leukemia in Venice,

her husband gone, she felt her own life flicker.
Somehow her forms assumed finer detail,
although she noticed actual things grow weaker,
their outlines vague. Searching for new soil,

she wandered to this country, where she saw,
in early spring, a branch of apricot
in bloom among stiff twigs. A week of sun
had undone heavy frost, and startled it.

Seeing the terraced valley, where small houses
were terra-cotta rectangles that shone
through haze, near ancient olive trees and fortresses,
she set about to cut resistive limestone

and red marble to life in the sarcophagi,
visions of tombs for her imagined kings;
she cut them into birth as unexpectedly
as violets spring from rock. "People and things

existed for me here in fabulous harmony,
so natural it seemed strange. Although the white
citrus trees and pines covered the land,
chapels and piers were never out of sight."

She smoothed a canvas skirt, her mica eyes
fastened on snow-covered mountain peaks. The task
of creating angular deities in friezes
was good. But still, occasionally, at dusk,

she said, she watched the steamboat from Varenna
furrow the lake, and hurried to the landing
to meet the boy whose death she'd dulled away
in those gray moments. She shuddered, recalling

sunsets obscured by vapor. "Only the chirr
of motors told me where I was. Mist fell,
and dimmed out the eroded planks, the pier's
geometry, lake scum, the rotted guard rail.

"Fog beckoned me. And also, as the south wind
moves, I brought an inner mist that blurred
or made my universe, although the mind
saved clearness for the work. One day I heard

San Giacomo's bells before I reached the wharf.
Purchasing wine and olives in a store,
I faltered; then, for all I scorned belief
(it was at vespers), I tugged at the door."

Cautious as a night marauder, stranger
to her first house, she stepped gingerly
behind bowed shoulders, found a bench and glanced
at the bone-white relic washed ashore and quietly

repaired, the soggy belly bleached, the pupils
glossed. Perhaps a craftsman from Bellano
had worked the piece some eighty years before,
and, when he had finished, saw wood glow.

Her neighbors had renewed the harrowed image
that had survived somehow. "A miracle,"
she said aloud, then halted at the one
word that meant too much, explained too little.

Watching a carpenter from Bergamo
turn to regard the model he had planed,
she saw at last her own figures as metaphors,
more alive than men, more dead than stone.

There, as the north wind rose up in the mountains,
she knew the statue had remained as limestone
and marble tombs are genuine. But then,
unlike those sculptures, her mortal son

was of a transient brightness, and could never
return, or be restored. Without repeating
those random thoughts, she never searched the pier
again for the dead child. Her story ending,

I knew volcanic tremors had ripped open
her eyes when that zinc-white log floated up here.
Her voice was fathoms down when she asserted,
"Christ rose on these shores, eleven years

ago, and on this day, the eve of Tenebrae
— the holy litany of gathering shadows —
this last week of Lent, before Good Friday
and the Great Vigil." Nodding at a yellow

primrose, she measured days as kilos verify
an infant's being, then said she saw light flare
through clouds long after dusk. She turned to me,
knowing I understood her words, and, more,

the truth of radiant images that rise,
unbidden, from the bottom of the mind's
dark waters, to survive whirlpools and surface,
mud-soaked, tattered, worn, to beach on sand,

bodiless, lake-drenched carriers of keenest
vision, loosened, when given legs and heads,
to clarify the mist, just as she freed
souls of those whose bodies she had made.

5

EL GRECO'S "ST. JAMES, THE LESS"

This moonlight fractured into mere threads of stars
shines now on eyes indifferent or turned to some
      white peak inside that none but he sees,
  he, and those taught by the painter's vision.

Light falls on blue-and-red robes whose shadows are
black mouths that cry of glare that has deepened them.
      One hand unfurls; its lambent fingers
  curve down then curl up, a torch upended.

That hand recalls a starburst that hung from a
white pine; it turned in altering light, and its
      green needles fell away and pointed at
  random, a fan on its branch, an uncertain omen.

One day a mourning dove that was stammering
faint notes flew low, splayed out like the tangle of
      white pine. The bird, the tree, and now that
  hand of St. James, are one form. The dove gone,

light stays, its glow the mind's brightness, gleam of a
first day on earth in tales of Creation when
      one beam that God devised, before the
  sun, would have shown us the world in one glance.

"STRAIGHT TALK, STRAIGHT AS THE GREEK"

(Ezra Pound and Hilda Doolittle, 1912)

Before he sent her poems — sea grasses, poppies,
hyacinths that stirred him — to Chicago,
he watched the branchy woman in the tearoom
of the British Museum, blond hair in bangs, lean body

draped in a kind of chiton, like Diana
carved in a stone relief. Her beauty's anchor
weighed him down: Was this the impetuous girl
with bonewhite hands, who scooped up fallen apples,

stroked maple leaves and found a lofty crow's nest
in Wyncote, Pennsylvania, only six years
before, only a century of moments
earlier, who uttered laconic phrases,

who held up arms to rain, who hurled herself
into high waves? If so, now, breakers calm,
she gave him sea-wind bearing her taut mind,
faint hepaticas that carried evening

and death, a harsh rose that held their love.
"Dryad," the name he'd given her, lived on
in her own whittled lines. He touched the rose,
recalled the chalky dryad, shut his eyes,

erased her name on the page and gave her another:
"H. D. Imagiste." Before he posted them,
he held them for a long time, listening
to a new wind scour flat rocks on a far shore.

CARRION

The chipmunk's carcass lay flat on a stone
stair that led to rooms above the shed.
Hind legs, a tail, a strand of wine-red beads
and innards, showed whose body it had been.

One step above the corpse, a cat discreetly
unfurled, with eyes half-closed, guarding the kill.
Caretakers had fed him well, and still
the animal had craved some swifter prey.

The cat himself, ill-used, had been abandoned.
Boarded at stables here to calm the horses,
he was released after the racing season
passed, and found a temporary place

on this estate. Later, he would be free
to forage in the woods. The horse he eased
"will make a good brood mare when her racing days
are done," the auctioneer said. Rings of grief:

Scissors, paper, rock, I sang as a child.
Scissors cuts paper that covers rock
that pulverizes scissors. Still I'm locked
in that small circle, flaying, being flayed.

Small fingers whipped my wrist: bland-mannered Catherine
was *paper*. I, being *rock*, would lash
my dearest Ann, with flimsy yellow hair,
for being *scissors*. So the wheel turned, and turns.

I touched the chipmunk's glittering cadaver,
then buried it. The cat quivered to stand,
warning my hand that stole the prize he murdered.
Beyond the steps, a spruce raised votive candles.

Walking through double rows of junipers
that day, I glanced away from cruelty,
or so I tried: a hawk warped in mid-air
called back the day I watched a herring gull

circle to land, scoop up a turtle, glide
upward again and drop it to crack its shell.
My neighbor shot the gardener who denied
he ever cared, and who was seen at Bill's

drinking bourbon with a new lover.
"She seemed too old, too stoical, for murder.
She won't get off," a villager asserted —
sadly, I thought. I never knew the killer,

had seen her only, taut as a dry leaf
someone had kicked on the ground, chilly, slight,
her skin worn porcelain, her long body
angular in stride, flexed, as in flight.

That night my feet, my elongated thighs
stiffened and went cold; then, as I lay
counting the stars, my carrion entrails
flickered below my eaten chest, my eyes.

THE LUXEMBOURG GARDENS

1. GUSTAVE FLAUBERT

The statue suits him: a sad oracle's
head rests on a pedestal that rises
from the shoulders of a bench, as if an angel
had scooped it up from the mud and flown it higher

than the park's fence. Viewing a wide allée
of horse-chestnut trees that, even now, pour
rain in sudden brightness, sly Flaubert
perches like an osprey above his prey.

No pigeon lights on his shadowy head
in blackening stone. As in Rouen, he tries
"to live in an ivory tower," but, indeed,
he finds "a tide of shit beats at its walls,"

an ebb-and-flow he scrutinized, as now.
Unlike his friend, George Sand, who reclines
on sunlit grass, some yards away, and glows
in white stone, closed book pressed to waistline,

he is made not to be seen, but to see:
facing him are chairs of green iron
on which, minutes ago, a man and a woman
had sat and glared, perhaps angrily.

"Speech is like a rolling machine that stretches
the feelings it expresses," Flaubert says,
then lets his eyes go vacant like the eyes
of a café-sitter who stares at passers-by

and focuses when a friend appears.
To see it all is to know the deepest layer,
and yet he must see everything. He lingers
now on a woman combing yellow hair,

and notices her chapped hands, baggy jeans,
then gazes at the walk. Screened by trees,
a mime in whiteface practices slow turns;
a man in gold-lace sandals ambles by;

a greyhound sniffs at an empty chair.
A *gardien* with a high hat scolds a vagrant
sprawled on the grass, then smiles at a *garde d'enfant*
wheeling a stroller, the arms of her sweater

knotted at her throat. The officer
looks up at the statue — jaw-length hair,
the moustache cut like a bow's streamers —
then strides away, as if he did not hear:

"Idols must not be touched; the gold paint
rubs off on our fingers." Stone ears take in
the crunch of polished patent leather
boots on the dirt path, the clack clack clack

of high-heeled shoes on a cobbled walk nearby.
I hide the leaf I stole to identify,
and know I am *his* subject, not he, mine.
I marvel at his keen glance. He replies:

"Nobody loves praise more than I, and praise
bores me." Searching for someone who would "practice
virtue without believing in it," he sees,
and his sight is love; he never loses

his critical remove, as does his Emma,
not even for a scarf that crooks like a huge gold comma
or the arc of a red ball that shines in flight,
catching the strong but tentative morning light.

2. THE GOOD WOMEN

Who caught them this way? Shapely stone
queens and other *grandes dames* lurk in trees,
cousins to the Statue of Liberty,
another classy vamp. They are made of contradiction:

Geneviève, a saint whose prayers saved Paris
from the invader, clenches her long fingers,
and peers through leaves,
                            round bosom, snaky braids;

Queen Matilda, Duchess of Normandy,
of the sword and crown, the cross and the fleur-de-lis,
rests the tall sword
                            against a narrow waist.

Waving a scepter, Queen Blanche of Castille,
who rescued the kingdom from rebels,
frees one hand
                            to clutch a billowing skirt,

while Charlemagne's mother, Bertha of the Great
Feet, holds her king, Pepin the Short,
and his throne
                            in her unsceptered hand

near fierce Queen Margaret of Anjou,
"She-wolf of France, and worse than wolves of France,"
who glides,
                            clasping her son to a curvy bodice,

and there is Hugo de Sade's wife, Laura de Noves,
possibly Petrarch's bold (here reticent) love,
beside Clémence Isaure,
                            who leans on one hip.

Under a wide-eyed Louise de Savoy,
who, not so simply, joined another queen
to arrange a peace treaty of Cambrai,
I slide into an iron chair, and frown

at an unseemly décolletage
some Beaux Arts sculptor dreamed had been the rage,
wrong, or at the least, chilly for court.
Then, as I leave, I watch a girl recite:

"*MARGUERITE DE FRANCE,*" Margaret
of Angoulême, Queen of Navarre, who wrote
tales that inspired Rabelais, and here —
                    (one hand touches the cheek, the other holds flowers)

coquette — allays my doubts: all oxymorons,
saints, muses, consorts, sages, scholars,
mothers of, daughters of, sirens, leaders,
flaming in paradox — those are the queens.

NOTES

FOOTSTEPS ON LOWER BROADWAY

Line 12: "I…headed for Pfaff's." Pfaff's Café. Charles Pfaff, owner; established 1856. In an interview, Whitman was quoted as having said: "I used to go to Pfaff's nearly every night." *The Brooklyn Daily Eagle*, 11 July 1866.

Stanza 4, lines 31 through 40: In March, 1842, Walt Whitman attended services twice at the Shearith Israel Synagogue on Crosby Street, between Spring and Broome, in Lower Manhattan. Recounting both visits in a newspaper, the *Aurora* (March 28-29), Whitman expressed wonder so intense as to show him at a loss for words. He wrote: "The heart within us felt awed as in the presence of memorials from an age that had passed away centuries ago. The strange and discordant tongue — the mystery, and all the associations that crowded themselves in troops upon our mind — made a thrilling sensation to creep through every nerve." Although Whitman does not refer to Judaism in his great poetic passages concerning world religions, he does incorporate Hebrew rhythms and imagery in his verse. Apparently the impact of Jewish ritual was deeper than he had supposed.

BESTIARIES

In "Animals," some creatures are freely adapted from Louis Ginzberg's *The Legends of the Jews*, Vol. l.
"They, Too," responds to Lewis Thomas' call, in *Lives of a Cell*, for a mythology of microbial beings.

RESCUE IN PESCALLO

According to local tales, a statue of Christ did wash up on the lake shore and was placed in a nearby church. However, the details here are entirely fictional.

Grace Schulman was born in New York City. She attended Bard College and the Johns Hopkins Writing Seminars, and received her M.A. and Ph.D. in English from New York University. Since 1972, she has been Poetry Editor of the *Nation*, and has taught at Baruch College, C.U.N.Y., where she is a professor of English. Schulman was Director of the Poetry Center, 92nd Street Y, from 1974 to 1984. The author of books of poems, translations, and criticism, she lives with her husband, Dr. Jerome L. Schulman, a scientist, in New York, and in East Hampton.

Poetry from The Sheep Meadow Press

Desire for White
Allen Afterman (1991)

Early Poems
Yehuda Amichai (1983)

Travels
Yehuda Amichai (1986)

Poems of Jerusalem and
Love Poems
Yehuda Amichai (1992)

Father Fisheye
Peter Balakian (1979)

Sad Days of Light
Peter Balakian (1983)

Reply from Wilderness Island
Peter Balakian (1988)

5 A.M. in Beijing
Willis Barnstone (1987)

Wheat Among Bones
Mary Baron (1979)

The Secrets of the Tribe
Chana Bloch (1980)

The Past Keeps Changing
Chana Bloch (1992)

Memories of Love
Bohdan Boychuk (1989)

Brothers, I Loved You All
Hayden Carruth (1978)

Selected Poems
Diana Der-Hovanessian (1994)

Orchard Lamps
Ivan Drach (1978)

A Full Heart
Edward Field (1977)

Stars in My Eyes
Edward Field (1978)

New and Selected Poems
Edward Field (1987)

Embodiment
Arthur Gregor (1982)

Secret Citizen
Arthur Gregor (1989)

The River Serpent and
Other Poems
Arthur Gregor (1994)

Nightwords
Samuel Hazo (1987)

Leaving the Door Open
David Ignatow (1984)

The Flaw
Yaedi Ignatow (1983)

The Ice Lizard
Judith Johnson (1992)

The Roman Quarry
David Jones (1981)

Claims
Shirley Kaufman (1984)

Summers of Vietnam
Mary Kinzie (1990)

The Wellfleet Whale
Stanley Kunitz (1983)

The Moonlit Upper Deckerina
Naomi Lazard (1977)

The Savantasse of Montparnasse
Allen Mandelbaum (1987)

The Landscape Is Behind the Door
Pierre Martory, translated by
John Ashbery (1994)

Other Titles from Sheep Meadow